Heaven in Your Heart
and in Your Pocket Too!

All the Best "99"
Ed Montgomery

Heaven in Your Heart and in Your Pocket Too!

KEYS TO ATTITUDE ELEVATION

DR. ED MONTGOMERY

CREATION HOUSE PRESS

HEAVEN IN YOUR HEART
AND IN YOUR POCKET TOO! by Ed Montgomery
Published by Creation House Press

Ed Montgomery
Abundant Life Cathedral
11230 Haruin Dr.
Houston, TX 77072

Unless otherwise noted, all Scripture quotations
are from the King James Version of the Bible.

Copyright © 1998 by Ed Montgomery
All rights reserved
ISBN: 0-88419-560-0
Library of Congress: 98-73619

89012345 BBG 87654321

Printed in the United States of America

CONTENTS

Introduction

Are you a dreamer? Have you ever imagined a better life for yourself, your family, and for those around you? Or have you consigned yourself to the "box" in life someone else has built for you.

This book is for those who will dare to peer over the sides of their mandated cubicles—to discover new horizons of who they truly are.

Chapter One

Why Can't I?
The American Dream

"Oh Beautiful, for spacious skies, for amber waves of grain.
For purple mountains majesty, above the fruited plain.
America, America, God shed his grace on thee,
And crowned thy good, with brotherhood, from sea to shining sea."

It's not where you are that counts—it's what you *do* where you are. But as quiet as it's kept, the "American Dream" for many, is nothing more than a frightening vision—a fairy tale with an unhappy ending.

So we must lift our thinking, blink our eyes, and alter our viewpoint. We must disrupt our perspective and change our paradigm, because wealth isn't limited to a place. To believe that it is, confines our thinking to a box. Don't you know that God gave us a planet? Even though our planet is a box, it is a box we won't soon out grow.

Boxes are the inventions of men—creations constructed according to the laws of mathematics, dimension and space. They're three-dimensional cubes, defined by length, width, and height, that provide perfect parameters for those who see in terms of limitations.

It doesn't matter how small or large the box is, it's still a box. Make it a square, rectangle, or any shape you will. Paint it, wrap it, or tie it in a bow. It's still a box. Those who predetermine the dimensions construct boxes. So show me a box and I'll show you limitations.

We're all born with box thinking. We were conceived within the boundaries of a box, called the womb. From the womb we emerge to be placed in another box called the crib, a place designed to protect us. Yet when we desire to get out, we also find it to be a place of confinement.

Now, confinement isn't always a bad thing; it provides us with a sense of security, well-being and safety. But inherent in the human spirit is the need to grow, the need to expand, and the need to transcend. We have an obligation to ourselves to be more than we presently are.

> **ATTITUDE KEY**
>
> *Your progress is determined by your dreams.*

Of course there are those who would have us remain satisfied with and in our box. So we're given toys . . . teddy bears, rubber ducks; and we're told to play. Millions of dollars are spent each year on "crib toys"— objects of fascination designed to keep an infant cooing and calm— playthings, designed to stop the crying that comes as the result of a desire for more.

Does this stop at the crib? No. We exist in a world that ushers us from one crib to another. We are crib creatures. From our cribs we are introduced to larger boxes: play pens, play rooms, nurseries, the front porch.

But does it stop there? No again. Before long we're introduced to kindergarten, home rooms, grade levels, and the institutions of higher learning. We graduate from what we think to be the last box, only to sit behind a desk in a mink-lined box called an office. So our bosses give us new crib toys: staplers, computers, telephones and family photos—all of which are intended to keep us merrily content from nine to five. Then to top it off, we're presented with a check at the end of the week for doing such a good "box job."

Some of us though, sooner or later, grasp the top edge of our box, and with all of our might pull ourselves up to curiously peep over the box's edge. And when we do, we are amazed. For there, beyond our box . . . is a whole new world! We look over our shoulder and peer downward. We scan the place we've pulled ourselves up from only to discover that it's smaller than the new sight we've seen over the top. Then that lightening fast computer called our brain calculates the comparison—and we come to the terrifying conclusion that there is a thing called "more."

ATTITUDE KEY

There is a thing called "more."

Knowing this, we struggle to hold on, but our strength fails us. We release our grip. We slide silently to the floor. But we are now no longer the same, because we've seen another world. Suddenly, we have caught the glimpse of an endless horizon. We now see others just like ourselves coming and going from box-to-box. And we ask the question, fatal to a prisoner's mentality: If *they* can get out of the box—why can't I?

WHY CAN'T I?

Why can't I? This is the most dangerous question in the world. There's no danger in asking it of the one in the box. But it is a dangerous proposition to those who created the box. Why?

Because *why* is the doorway to *who* am I? *Who* put me here? Who are those beyond my confinement?

The question of *who* then leads us to *what*—what am I doing here? what am I accomplishing? What will become of my future?

> **ATTITUDE KEY**
>
> *Rise above your problem, and you will find yourself high enough to see the solution.*

But unfortunately, we all too often just shrug our shoulders and content ourselves once again within our little box. We fondle our crib toys and resign ourselves to our lot in life. But our crisis is far from over, because we have asked, why, who, and what. You'd think the process would stop there. And it may, for a while. After all, these are silent questions asked in the privacy of our own minds. But once they've been asked, the seed has been planted.

Our memories are like priceless cameras with wide-angle lenses. So once we capture the images outside of our box, they can prod and irritate us. They invade our dreams, sometimes cloaking themselves as nightmares, then flash themselves to the forefront of our daydreams. Consequently, we become disenchanted with our box. Instead of a place of security, it soon becomes our prison.

> **ATTITUDE KEY**
>
> *Having faith makes nothing easy—it just makes things possible.*

It is then that our silent screams of frustration percolate into continuous geysers of need. Suddenly, we need to get away, we need to get out, we need more—we need to change!

And now, we have a problem. Because why, who, and what have posed a new question: *how* . . . how can I leave this place?

Chapter Two

Don't Box Me In

Have you ever wondered, *How did I get into this rut?* Ruts are boxes. We get into them by allowing ourselves to be told what to think, what to do, where to go, where to live, and how much money we can make. These are all boxes.

Boxes are the products of people. And whoever is in charge decides how we "common people" should live. (A little sarcasm, I admit it.) But our destinies are all too often determined by the present thought and worldview of the prevailing culture. This has always been the case.

I recently read a passage in the Bible that changed my way of thinking forever. I was reading the story of how the ancient Jewish people came into the institution of slavery under the cruel hand of the Egyptians.*

The passage reads, ". . . there arose a new king over Egypt . . . and he said to his people, look, the people of the children of Israel are *more* and *mightier* than we; come, let us deal *shrewdly* with them . . . therefore they set taskmasters over them to afflict them."

*Exodus chapter 1.

Now any other time, I would have considered this to be merely the telling of a nice Bible story. But there is an interesting point to this. Notice, the Hebrew people were actually greater in number than the Egyptians. Not only that, but they were also stronger. How could Egypt have possibly enslaved them? That would be like one man fighting in the ring with thirty experienced boxers. Enslavement should have been impossible!

Ah, but here's the key: Egypt didn't use force until they convinced the Hebrews that Egypt was mightier. This was such a con game! A scheme! The oldest trick in the book! Convince your opponent you are stronger than they are by attacking them first. Consequently, the young Jewish nation was enslaved by the belief that they were inferior.

INFERIORITY

To believe a product is inferior, is to believe there was a mistake on the part of the manufacturer when making it. This isn't difficult to understand. We send products back to manufacturers all the time—and this type of thinking makes sense, when it comes to things. But when it involves people—it makes no sense at all.

The Creator never has, and never will make an inferior person. Of course we all probably know people we would gladly send back, but that's not because of a production flaw. Difficult people are the product of their own thinking and choices.

Every person sent to this planet has a reason for being here. The limitations they must deal with don't matter. We all deal with them. Some must overcome physical, mental and emotional limitations. Some are confined to wheelchairs because of disabilities and physical challenges which make life difficult to say the least. Some are viewed by the majority of a culture as undesirable because of the color of their skin or a belief system they have chosen.

> **ATTITUDE KEY**
>
> *The key to unlock the box you're in, is not in someone else's pocket—it's within your own mind.*

But, God has a plan for each of us and we must all make a contribution to the society around us. The world wouldn't be the same place without us.

So no person in the sight of God is inferior. Believe this truth about others, and believe it about yourself. To do the opposite is lethal to who you are!

We all must see our box for what it is—just a box. If it has dimensions, know that someone designed it. If you feel locked in, know that someone has shut the door. If you keep screaming for release, know that someone hears you, even if they refuse to unlock the door. If you want out, know that the key to the lock isn't in someone else's pocket—it is within your own mind. And it's been there all along.

HAVE A BATTLE PLAN

I'm what you call an old movie buff. I especially love the old blood and guts war movies. In many of these pictures, you will notice that while the troops are fighting, the General is usually perched high atop a hill watching the outcome of the battle. When I first noticed this, I thought to myself, how dare he remain in the safety of distance while his men are dying at his command. But then I thought about it. It's very difficult to develop a strategy while fighting on the front line. You can't see the whole picture from there.

So it is with getting out of boxes. We must be able to determine what they are before we can understand how to get out of them.

If you are one of the few who still believe racism is not a problem, then I have a bridge to sell you in Brooklyn! Racism is the greatest sin of American society. No greater box has ever been built than the box of racism. It is considered to be America's dirty little secret. But the secret is out!

> **ATTITUDE KEY**
>
> *The creator of the universe has given you an "A" in life, but it's up to you to keep it.*

Do you have you any idea what it feels like to grow up in an America where you're told that you must be twice as good as your white counterparts? Can you imagine the psychological damage that has been done? An entire race of people has long strained themselves under the burden of having to "be better." They must be better doctors, better lawyers, better preachers, and better teachers. Of course this drive for excellence is producing a work force in our nation that is second to none. But to have to believe you must be twice as good, leaves one with the impression that what you presently are, isn't good enough. And what's the standard? The color of one's skin.

Judging someone by the color of their skin is a box. It is a box that millions live within every day of their lives. And it goes back to the con of the Egyptian Pharaohs to somehow convince a people they aren't quite good enough—not up to standard—not up to par.

However, millions of African Americans have peered over the edge of this box. They've seen what their world holds for them. The present racial conflict we're experiencing in America is the result of people who are simply sick of their boxes. They're knocking down the walls, climbing over the edge, and refusing to remain content in their places.

The Color Box

As we rush forward to the twenty-first century, expect to hear the sound of collapsing boxes all across America. It is a loud, disturbing, disruptive sound. But don't be alarmed, because it is the sound of freedom. It's the sound of those who are learning to be content with who and what they are. You will hear them striving to be twice as good, not because there is some color standard to meet, but because they're in competition with themselves. You see, the only box we should ever have to worry about, is the box we create for ourselves.

Believing in God isn't synonymous with believing that we should live in poverty. Unfortunately, some in the world lift high the virtues of poverty. Those who do, have probably never been poor.

It's very easy to preach that others shouldn't concern themselves with money when you have it or have had it at one time. It's not money that corrupts, it's the attitude of the person who possesses it. There is a difference between having money, and money having you. So don't fall for it!

To put this in perspective: it's not that we all seek to be rich, we only seek to be secure. "Rich" is how we view financial security. But it doesn't take millions to have all that we need. Most of us just want to be able to pay the light bill and house note on time, drive the kind of car we desire, put our kids through college, and have a decent amount left for retirement. We want to feel the security of knowing that if we lost our jobs at anytime, we could live worry-free until we found another one. We want the security of knowing if anything went wrong, our families wouldn't have to suffer. We don't want to be entombed in the poverty box.

This isn't very much to ask. You know it, I know it, and God knows it. So the poverty box is one I refuse to remain in.

We're taught in the Bible to love others, as we love ourselves. No truer words can ever be spoken. But, others will never be loved properly until we learn to love ourselves properly. So we need to reject the rejection box.

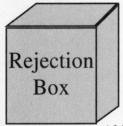

Love of self is not some narcissistic sickness. It's vital to our mental and spiritual health. So the first thing God did in my life was convince me of His love for me. Because it is only when I believe I am loved that I will discover the fact that I'm lovable. Although this simple fact can sometimes take years to get across, being lovable enables me to accept the fact that it's okay to accept love from others, and even from myself. When I can love myself, I become accepting of other people. I'm at peace with myself and with others.

It doesn't matter who doesn't love me or who never

gave me love in the past. I can't survive in this box. What matters, is who loves me now! Because God doesn't reject me, I can stop rejecting others—and get out of this box.

Racism, poverty, and rejection are boxes built by man. However we end up there—we don't have to stay boxed in.

ATTITUDE KEY

You have been called to break free ... to break out. You have been chosen to shake the chains that hold you within the walls of impossibilities.

Chapter Three

Endless Horizons

Independence is a satisfying state. There's no more satisfying feeling than the one that comes through knowing you are free of the manipulative strings of someone else. It feels good to be out of the box.

We have now started what few would even dare to try by pulling ourselves up and over the edge of our box. Our inner strength has done it's job. We're spectacular creatures, and there's reason to celebrate. But it is illusion to believe accomplishments are the product of us—and us alone.

We took pride as a toddler in the fact that we could walk. But have we forgotten that before we could walk, we had to first learn how to stand? Remember how you grabbed on to an object and pulled yourself up? Who put that object there in the first place?

The truth of the matter is, someone helped us stand. So we really aren't as *independent* as we are *interdependent.* Someone was there before us, watching over our first steps.

Let me to tell you about Buddy. Buddy was a bright, energetic, enterprising kid. But these characteristics were latent and well hidden behind Buddy's quietness. I would even go so far as to say that Buddy was shy. Not very shy, but shy enough to keep him from revealing his real abilities.

> **ATTITUDE KEY**
>
> *Possibilities are the product of perspective.*

When Buddy was fourteen, he joined the Boy Scouts of America. He started as a Cub Scout and achieved every award the Cub Scouts had to offer. So there was no place for Buddy to go but up. Yet Buddy was limited to the confines of his background. Buddy was a black kid growing up in the heat of the American Civil Rights movement.

The Boy Scouts of America decided they had to do their part. So they invested block grants and private donations into the youth of inner-cities ravaged by riots. The Boy Scouts would choose those who had achieved at least the rank of Star (a ranking system based on the acquiring of merit badges) for a special program. And Buddy was one of those chosen.

The program selected high-ranking Scouts from various troops within a city, flew them to the National Jamboree in Idaho, and on the way visited some of America's national landmarks. The Boy Scouts would pay the greater portion of the expenses while the sponsoring organization would pay the rest. So Buddy's church and community got together to send two of it's best scouts on the trip—and Buddy was one of them.

Because of this opportunity, Buddy took his first plane ride, saw Pike's Peak, visited British Columbia, and met other Scouts from around the world. He heard a smorgasbord of languages, discussed the difference between various cultures, and joined hands with others

of different races. After this, Buddy returned to his hometown socially illuminated.

> **ATTITUDE KEY**
>
> *We will never venture beyond the boundaries of our preset limitations without the vision of something greater.*

For years, Buddy never gave much thought to his trip. After all, it was just a trip, a memory. But at the age of seventeen, Buddy began to dream. He dreamed of traveling around the world. He looked forward to the day he could see other places and engage new people. And today, Buddy travels when and wherever he wants. He motivates people to break out of their boxes and achieve the dreams that are in their hearts. Buddy is independent. And it was the Boy Scouts and his community that gave him a peek over the edge of the box.

GIVE SOMEONE AN ENDLESS HORIZON AND THEY WILL TRAVEL FAR

Buddy teaches us that possibilities are the product of perspective. We will never venture beyond the boundaries of present limitations without the vision of something greater. So we must first become aware that there is something more.

We see it every day in the world of advertising. Tune in your radios and television sets, or pick up a magazine or newspaper. Millions are spent every thirty seconds to promote a product. Do we need the product? Who cares? Is it a good product? That's irrelevant! It doesn't matter what the product is, who needs it, or whether it's useful or not. Because advertising is the processes in which need, usefulness, and desire is created.

Many of the best inventions in the world have gone unnoticed because we've never heard about them. Our styles of clothes, the kinds of cars we drive, and the toothpaste we use, find themselves in our possession because of advertising. Advertising is promoted information.

But there will always be those in our world who would keep us ignorant. They would have us believe nothing exists outside of our box beyond what we presently have.

> **ATTITUDE KEY**
>
> *There is a breakthrough on your horizon.*

Yet, beyond your box is a brand new world. There are things to see, places you've never dreamed of going, and people you've never met. What a shame to live out our lives in the box of another's understanding of life.

Let us break away from those who would confine us to what they think we should do or ought to be. We're more than a resident of a community, city, state or country. We're citizens of the world. There are planes to catch and oceans to cross.

> **ATTITUDE KEY**
>
> *Beyond your box is a brand new horizon.*

We daily exist in our own tiny cubicle amid a vast universe—but there is more. Search out the information for yourself. By doing so, you will expand your vision and change your world.

Chapter Four

The Tail of the Silver Monkey

J ack was awakened by the high pitched shrill of who-knows-what! So many possibilities awaited them in the South American jungle. Their bones ached. How much farther would they have to travel? The brush covered trail left by some ancient civilization led them deeper into the bush and seemed to close behind them with every hopeful step.

Morning had dawned. The sun, round and golden, was peeking through the tree leaves. It was time to pack up and get moving. Today would be the day. The expedition should reach its destination before sunset. That is, barring any complications.

They had been walking for hours and the perspiration was drawing insects like bees drawn to a honeycomb. How much more of this could they take?

Then, suddenly, it was there, the sacred Temple of Lochela. Legend assured them that inside they would find their treasure—the Silver Monkey.

The temple was finally in sight, and Jack recalled the ancient writings which had started him on his quest. As the story goes, the Silver Monkey guarded the sacred tombs of the legendary Lochelation kings. Now that they had found them, they would be rich— wealth beyond imagination! Just a few more steps and it would all be theirs.

In the clearing straight ahead they could see the tomb entrance guarded by the fabled idol. There it was—the Silver Monkey. Finally, the search was over. Jack approached the pedestal of the relic with reverence. He reached out as a church-like hush invaded their space and touched the statue, stroking its back. Then, with one swift movement, he pushed down hard on the idol's tail. It was a lever! And as it clicked into place, a slab of solid stone began to rise behind the pedestal like curtains on a play's opening night. It revealed an etching of script. A language long forgotten. Armand, the ancient language scholar of the group, brushed centuries of dust from the encryption and translated for the group. It read:

> *He who finds this wall of words,*
> *Has found the secret of the key.*
> *For wealth beyond your wildest*
> *dreams, is buried five miles deep.*

Jack bristled, "Five miles deep? What?! It would take years to uncover this treasure with the tools we have. We would need bulldozers, jackhammers, and a team of at least ten men," he argued. Jack knew that even with the proper tools, it could take months. So he dropped his head in anguish and frustratedly said, "Oh God! To be so close and now this!"

Jack released the tail of the Silver Monkey and watched the wall of words shroud itself once more with the slab of stone. Then Jack's team left the shrine and headed home. As they left the tomb, they could almost hear the laughter of the ancient kings. Their treasure would remain a secret for yet another generation.

What they didn't know was, the treasure was buried only five feet beyond the wall. Five feet! It would have taken thirty minutes or so to retrieve the treasure with a pick and shovel. It seems the mysterious ancients were only willing to share their prize with those who had the will to dig—those who would at least try. But because Jack was unwilling to commit to the hard work and struggle the ancients described, he refused himself the surprise of early success.

How often have so many others waited for some deity to pour out great blessings of wealth without any effort on their part? To wait for some higher power to give us anything is the first indication of weakness. We were never created to receive without effort, to gain without trying, or to achieve without struggle.

> **ATTITUDE KEY**
>
> *There is nothing unholy about struggle.*

STRUGGLE

There is nothing unholy about struggle. Oh, I know the Christian community is saturated with the widespread belief that struggling for something is a sign that God doesn't want you to have it. But that's not quite true. This kind of thinking is for those who have never had to struggle for anything.

My grandfather worked two jobs just to keep his family fed. It was from him that I learned the value of struggle. I learned there is something sacred about going after what you want and not giving up until you get it. Difficulty isn't a sign that God has forsaken you. To the contrary, difficulty is actually a sign that something wonderful is waiting on the other side. Struggle is about courage, it's about endurance, and it's about faith. Faith refuses to waver in the face of difficulty. It's knowing, even when you're traveling in the wrong direction, that all things will work for your good.

ATTITUDE KEY

Struggle is about courage.

God is on the side of those who struggle. For without struggle, there is no progress. Our prize may only be five feet away, but we will never know it until we start digging.

POWER IS GUARDED BY PROBLEMS

Years ago, before video games were common in the home, they were played mostly in arcades. One of the first and most popular was a game called PacMan.

PacMan was a tiny, circular, smiley face with a ferocious appetite. His goal was to evade his approaching enemies, while searching for the power pill at the same time. Devouring the power pill would empower PacMan to become stronger than his enemies, enabling him to turn on them and consume them at will. The only problem was, his enemies guarded the power pill and could destroy PacMan's pursuits. You would spend a pocket-full of quarters until you developed a winning strategy to make PacMan win. So even with this silly game, there was a price to be paid to ensure a win.

No worthwhile goal is ever easy. If it was, everybody would achieve their goals without effort. The rewards of life are never handed over without a fight. You will find that anything worth having, is in the possession of someone else, and they're not going to give it up just because you want it.

This tells us something very valuable. If something is very difficult to obtain, it is most likely very valuable. So we can be assured that our efforts won't be wasted.

Therefore, don't fear the problem that seems to block your goal. Don't be afraid to struggle. Don't be afraid to work. When you reach the tail of your silver monkey, refuse to listen to the naysayers,

> **ATTITUDE KEY**
>
> *You must dig for what you desire.*

and start to dig. The reward you receive as you commit to your goal will be well worth the fight.

Chapter Five

1-900-PSYCHIC

The pungent odor of volcanic ash is almost unbearable. Nature has taken a recess—the wind is still. There is no sound of singing birds, ocean waves crashing against distant rocks, or the rustle of leaves dancing to the touch of a breeze. You are flanked by the inhabitants of a remote village, situated on a tropical island. The culture has never been touched by the beliefs and traditions of any other civilization. They are bound by their own traditions, which have been passed down for hundreds—maybe thousands—of years.

The ceremony begins. It is the yearly rite of sacrifice. As you stand amazed at the sight, a virgin is about to make her contribution to the future prosperity of her people. She is clothed in white—bound hand and foot. Your tour guide reveals she is from the finest of families. At the signal of the tribal chief, she will be carried to the mouth of a seething volcano and flung helplessly in into its molten core. Then for seven days, the village will engage in food and dance. The gods of prosperity will have been appeased, and the village will again be safe from poverty and ruin.

You are breathless. How can this be? Such a cruel act of inhumanity. Such ignorance and backwardness. This type of thinking would never be tolerated in civilization.

But it's all around us. Think about it. With all of our computers, modems, and all of our high tech and high yield CD's, deep in the back room of the minds of our well-educated society, is the belief in magic.

Of course we would never admit to virgins in volcanoes, but we also have our share of ancient rituals. They range from lotteries to psychics. Fortune telling is big business on television today. And for many prominent celebrities, it has become a very lucrative source of income. What gives? Are we a society branded with an "instant winner" mentality?

Somewhere in the remote regions of our minds we harbor hopes that some deity, some power from beyond . . . will somehow smile upon our little corner of the world. "Rain upon us riches beyond compare O god of instant success!" We find this thinking among the common, the rich, the faithless, and the religious in our well-educated society.

> **ATTITUDE KEY**
>
> *Wealth is not a matter of accident.*

Wealth is not a matter of accident. God doesn't smile on the income of some while frustrating the efforts of others. Increase is not a matter of chance—it is a matter of perception.

You are a unique creation. You were methodically and wonderfully made, and you have the ability to transform and transcend any situation. You are the conqueror of devastating odds and the possessor of your own destiny. Your greatest asset is not around or above you, it is deep within you. You can change your environment by merely changing yourself.

Just as Adam blamed Eve for their problems in the garden*, so we find ourselves similarly blaming others for the misfortunes in our lives. Please don't misunderstand me. I am very much aware of how lies, vicious rumors, false testimonies and spurious charges can greatly alter anyone's life. There are innocent people in jail right now because of some incompetent lawyer or evidence that was twisted to give the appearance of truth. Countless thousands have been denied jobs and advancement of careers solely because of past indiscretions, convictions and mistakes.

It doesn't matter to society that the past is the past. People judge you based on what they perceive you to be.

But this just proves my point all the more. We can't depend on other people to promote, prosper, or provide for us. People may help us, but we can't come to expect this help in our daily experiences. Is this cynicism? Not really. Is it realism?—you bet!

We must learn to depend on ourselves and the God given tal-

> **ATTITUDE KEY**
>
> *You are the conqueror of devastating odds, and the possessor of your own destiny.*

ents that reside within in each of us. Every one of us have been graced with divine gifts. No human being has come into this world without the seeds of ability planted deep within. It is the knowledge of these seeds that creates our inner-hunger to accomplish more, to expect more, and to believe we deserve more.

*Genesis 2.

This may sound blasphemous to the religious, but if you take the time to really think about it, it isn't blasphemous at all. In some ways, one of our greatest handicaps is our dependence upon God—rather than our dependence upon the God within us. For too long, we have left ourselves out of the equation and have found ourselves looking upward toward the sky rather than inward toward our hearts.

ATTITUDE KEY

Your greatest asset is not around, but deep within you.

One of the greatest passages I've ever read is found in the Bible, in 2 Corinthians 3:9. It says, ". . . we are God's fellow workers . . . God's field." We are in this thing as deep as God is. We aren't some outsiders looking in while God magically fixes our lives. We have a stake in this thing too! We must respond to the urges and gentle nudging of God's voice within ourselves. What victory is there unless God can accomplished something . . . not just *for* us, but *through* us?

Every time we succeed against impossible odds, we prove the availability of the power of God within us. We prove to the universe and every force of good and evil, that God was quite sane when He created us.

How silly to believe that virgins in a volcano can somehow stem the tide of unwanted circumstances. But that is really no more silly than believing our prosperity is based on a throw of the dice, a turn of the wheel of fortune, or some TV Psychic who is only going to tell you what they (for a price) think you want to hear. There is more to this than meets the eye. Sophisticated voodoo is still voodoo.

Chapter Six

The Genius Screaming to Get Out of You

Every year during the Christmas holidays, I look forward to grabbing a cup of hot cocoa, curling up in my favorite chair, positioning my feet comfortably on the ottoman, and watching the seasonal presentation of *It's A Wonderful Life* on television. James Stewart is very convincing as the depressed owner of a debt-ridden Savings and Loan, who believes the world would be better off if he didn't exist. In the story, an angel helps restore his faith by showing him that life matters, and that the world would actually be worse off without him.

I believe each of us is on this planet for a reason. It is no accident or coincidence that we have emerged at this time. Although some parents may consider our birth an accident, that doesn't make it true. Our parents are merely the conveyor belt through which we were delivered. We existed in the womb of God

> **ATTITUDE KEY**
>
> *Sometimes, you can change your environment by merely changing your friends.*

long before we were born.

You see, our entrance upon planet earth wasn't the beginning of our life. God is eternal, and eternity has no end or beginning. It just is. Every act, every thought, and every imagination originates in God. In God, there is no past or future, only the present. So we were in God, long before He willed us into our present generation.

God has a plan for this planet, and we are a crucial part of that plan. It makes no difference how we got here or who our natural parents are. You could have been a test tube baby. Out of millions of sperm, you were the sperm that succeeded, and God has a plan for your life.

> **ATTITUDE KEY**
>
> *Prosperity is not the state of your pocketbook— it is a matter of your heart.*

God planned our entry onto the stage of life at just the right scene. We have a character that must come to life in this play, with lines to be spoken at just the precise moment. As a matter of fact, without our spoken lines, the play can't continue without making drastic adjustments. The other characters must hear our lines as a cue to when they say theirs. So, we are crucial to the plan of God. We belong here.

Each of us has a contribution to make on this planet. We may not know what it is, but we'll find out. It will be revealed to us at the proper time. It may take years, but our ultimate purpose for being will be revealed. So, let's prepare.

We prepare our children for school with school supplies. A carpenter needs his hammer. An architect needs her drafting board. For a doctor to walk into an operating room without a scalpel is to be unprepared.

Our Creator is the greatest of planners—a master of strategy—an organizer of detail. So it would be uncharacteristically negligent of Him to send His creation into a harsh environment without the necessary equipment to aid them in fulfilling their task.

Therefore, God has equipped us with gifts—talents—and abilities. He placed them within us. We may not recognize them, but they're there.

THE HIDDEN POTENTIAL WITHIN YOU

The human spirit is rich soil. It is a nutrient-loaded field replete with the promises of a future harvest. It is vast and unfathomable, the resting-place of dormant potential.

Deep within the womb of the human spirit, God has chosen to hide His seed. He has chosen to deposit every tool you will ever need to succeed on this planet in the vault of your spirit. Each seed is like a time-released capsule—a preappointed moment—in which it is designed to explode. "Every good and perfect (complete) gift is from above . . . " (James 1:17).

God uses seed form to store your potential.

So, who are you? What are you? What is it that you have to offer this world? What are your gifts?

Is there a book within you begging to be written?

Or a new philosophy of education clamoring to be revealed?

An invention destined to change the quality of life throughout the world?

A championship athlete?

A trainer of championship athletes?

The catalyst to church revival?

New corporate structures?
The presidency of your Parent-Teachers Organization?

> **ATTITUDE KEY**
>
> *Increase the places in your heart, and a full pocketbook won't be far behind.*

Every child born has been given a gift powerful enough to change the world around it. Isn't it awesome to realize the world is waiting for you?

How tragic it is to watch gifted, talented individuals pervert their gifts through crime, gangs, and immoral lifestyles. If we could only see ourselves as God sees us, we would savor every second we have on this planet.

YOU HAVE ALL YOU NEED

"... for it is He that giveth thee power to get wealth ..."
—Deuteronomy 8:18

Again, wealth doesn't fall from the sky. Nor does some angel make daily special deliveries! It is this kind of thinking that makes a person appear very spiritual while living on welfare!

It's possible to be a very religious person and starve to death! Often we see news reports telling of starvation in a foreign country, or of children dying for lack of medical care. We hear of families living under bridges right here in the prosperous USA. Our minds flood with questions. How can this be? If there is a God, why doesn't He stop it?

The truth of the matter is, God has already given each of us the resources we need to make sure these type of things never happen. The problem is in the hearts of men. When the human race no longer shows kindness and compassion to their fellow man, we see the effects of evil.

I'm quite sure God could change it with a wave of His hand. But God has given the rule of this planet to man. God has given man the will to choose, and He won't disturb the delicate balance of things.

But God isn't idle. He has chosen to function through the vehicle of the hearts of men and women—the place where He deposited gifts, talents, and abilities.

Everything we need is already within us. We have been given the power (ability) to get wealth. God has chosen to put our greatest commodity within us.

MONEY

Millionaires have a different perspective on wealth. They gain and lose millions all the time. Money to them is merely a tool. When we understand money, we begin to understand how God blesses us.

There is a difference between currency and money. Currency is the paper and coin minted by a particular country. Money, however, is a medium of exchange. If we lived in a society where eggs were the national currency, we would find that the people with the most money, would be the people with the most chickens! So money can come in many different forms.

When you look for a job, in your mind is the question of how much you will make. When you agree to take the job, you also agree to trade an hour of who you are (notice I said who you are), for what the company agrees to pay. You trade an hour of your time, talent, ability and energy, for a certain amount of money.

TIME + TALENT + ABILITY + ENERGY= $MONEY$

When you receive your paycheck at the end of the week, you hold in your hand *time, talent, ability, and energy*—in suspended animation. Currency is all of these qualities in a tangible form.

Have you ever heard the saying, "Time is money"? Sure you have, and it's true. Not only is time money—life is money! You spend a portion of your life for the money you earn. No one gives you a paycheck—you earn it! You earn it by trading a portion of your life that you'll never see again. The only way you can account for it is by the amount of currency you receive.

Every time you go to the supermarket, you exchange a portion of your life for food. Every time you pay your mortgage, buy a car, pay a bill—you've exchanged a portion of your life.

On the down side, every time a person purchases drugs, alcohol, or substances to abuse their bodies, they have exchanged a portion of their lives for that which will destroy them. To steal from someone is to take a portion of his or her life.

On the up side, every time a person assists another who can't help themselves breathes a portion of their life into theirs.

So there is a genius inside of you screaming to get out. You have been given great gifts. But it is up to you to use them wisely. This genius is you; not some fake pretending to be you. It is the real you, the you without the influence of friends, enemies, or those who think you don't have it in you.

> **ATTITUDE KEY**
>
> *The fortune of the fearful is lack—but the destiny of the faithful is abundance.*

This genius knows what he wants. It knows the gifting inside. It has dreams, visions, and lofty goals. And if given a chance, it will accomplish exactly what it is suited to do with sparkling success.

The genius in you is begging, crying—screaming to get out! It wants to be everything you can possibly be. So release your genius. There is absolutely no use in letting such good talent go to waste.

Chapter Seven

Heaven in Your Heart

What is your most valuable commodity? What possession do you hold dear? Is it your bank account, career, house, vehicle? Maybe it's your family . . . your children . . .? You've worked for these things. You've given your time and perspiration to make them work. Whatever or whoever your most valuable commodity is, you consider it important enough to maintain and nurture.

> **ATTITUDE KEY**
>
> *Faith allows you to see the silver lining you were never able to see before.*

Of course, our relationships with our families and friends are of inestimable value. But *things,* whether material or personal, are also considered to be items of value. Yes, you value them. They occupy a special place in your life. And contrary to some religious beliefs, it's all right to hold these things as important.

How interesting that the Bible spends so much time talking about material possessions. We've all heard the arguments about whether

Jesus was rich or poor. Some say that since He was poor, we should strive to live a life below the poverty line. But the issue isn't whether Jesus was rich or poor. The issue is—what does Jesus say about money?

In the Bible, there is a passage that reads: "Lay not up for yourselves treasures upon earth, where moth and rust doth corrupt, and where thieves break through and steal: But lay up for yourselves treasures in heaven, where neither moth nor rust doth corrupt, and where thieves do not break through nor steal: For where your treasure is, there will your heart be also."*

We've probably heard this saying, "Lay up for yourselves treasures in heaven . . . " a thousand times. It's a grand saying. The words invoke a sense of security. We all want and need to know that what we possess is safe and secure. But, the question is: How can we possibly get treasure stored up in heaven?

No place on this planet seems safe nowadays. But heaven is a long way away. I've never been there, and I know the most common way of getting there is through death. So the idea of laying up treasures there seems sort of like putting your money in an eternal Certificate of Deposit.

ATTITUDE KEY

Welcome change, for it will usher you into brave new worlds.

However, the treasures being talked about in this Bible passage are evidently vulnerable to moth, rust and thieves. So they must be real, honest-to-goodness, material goods! Goods that can be corrupted, destroyed and stolen. The Bible says we are to ". . . lay up treasures in heaven . . .," and that by doing so, we will be able to keep our possessions safe and sound. This sounds wonderful! Heaven must be the safest place anywhere.

*Matthew 6:19-21.

But again, how do we deposit this week's paycheck in heaven? Heaven is a spiritual place.

This conflict drove me to search out the real meaning of this passage, because this direct quote of Jesus has more meaning to it than meets the eye. But before we can fully get an understanding of this quote, we must define some terms.

HEAVEN

You've probably heard the saying, "Everyone wants to go to heaven but nobody wants to die!" Heaven is considered the land of flowing milk and honey—pearly white gates, streets of gold, and mansions dotting the horizon. It's a place of eternal bliss and undisturbed happiness.

If you were to ask any ordinary person on the street about heaven, the answer you'd receive would probably be similar to the description above. So we all have our own ideas about heaven. But there is something far deeper than heaven's "place."

Now of course, I'm not contradicting the existence of the place called heaven. I'm merely dealing with the concept of it. The Bible defines heaven as ". . . the vaulted expanse of the sky . . . the seat of order of things eternal and consummately perfect where God dwells with other heavenly beings . . . the home of the saints."

The apostle John claims to have seen heaven, while the apostle Paul talks of being taken up to it either in or out body, he didn't know. Some look for it in the northern sky while others believe it to be on some distant planet. But regardless of the various opinions, one view remains constant: heaven is considered the place where God lives. And this is the basis of our dilemma.

HEAVEN BELONGS TO GOD

God is omnipresent. He is everywhere at the same time. God is the "Beginning and End, the First and Last, and the Past and Future."

Some have said that God doesn't exist, and, in a sense, they're right. For God to merely exist, He would have to be confined to the limitations of existence. But God created the height, length, breadth, and depth of existence. He is everywhere always, transcendent of time. So God is beyond mere existence. He lives according to His own power.

ATTITUDE KEY

Change is the mid-wife prepared to help you birth new experiences.

However, this doesn't mean that God created Himself. Because for God to have created Himself would have required His existence *before* Himself to make His own creation possible. Consequently, where man in his finite understanding is able to comprehend the infinite, we acquiesce to the announcement, that God just is.

In light of the greatness of God, what person or place can completely contain Him? God is greater than the earth, greater than the galaxy, greater than the entire universe.

I'm reminded of the old brain twister that asks, "Can God create a rock too large for Him to move?" The answer is yes, of course. But He wouldn't do it— because He is also omniscient or all-knowing, and perfect wisdom would dictate not to do it.

God created the heavens and the earth. So to take this a little further, could God create a heaven so large that it could completely house Him? Of course He could. However, God isn't completely contained by any one object because all things are *in* Him.

Several years ago, I shocked a group of people by saying I had no plans of going to heaven. After a great space of silence, I then quoted a passage of Scripture from the Bible stating the soul that comes from God goes back to Him. I continued by saying, "My plan is to get back to God!"

Therefore, since God doesn't exist within the confines of something greater than Himself, it stands to reason that He doesn't live in heaven—heaven lives in Him! So going to God is also going to heaven. For wherever God is, there you'll find heaven.

> **ATTITUDE KEY**
>
> *Your goals have the power to pull you—push you—and to promote you.*

THE GREATEST REVELATION

God wastes nothing. He leaves nothing to chance. He scatters nothing on the ground or beside the road as an enticement to scavengers seeking what they don't earn. He is protective of His gifts, for they come from the depths of His creative soul. God's gifts are free for the asking, but they aren't cheap.

There is order and procedure in God's realm. So to receive the best He has to offer, requires the best we have to offer. God has hidden the best in you, wrapped it as a loving parent, and awaits your Christmas morn expression as you discover your gift. He will tolerate no schemes, tricks, or cons. God guards that which

He has designed for your benefit. He frustrates the feeble attempt of thieves who would rob you of your inheritance. Therefore, God placed your wealth in the safest place possible—your heart, your inner self, the core of who you really are.

THE SCAVENGERS OF MEN'S SOULS

> **ATTITUDE KEY**
>
> *Set your goals high and watch them propel you to places you've never been to before.*

Our world is filled with voices. Voices that call, voices that entice, voices that seduce. Everywhere we turn, we are confronted with the siren sounds of those who would prey upon our treasures. We are rich and they know it—the enemies of our souls. They desire to stuff themselves full with the succulent manna of our gifts. They long to drink from us, quenching their thirst with the nectar of our creative powers.

Our enemies are real, yet you won't find them cloaked in flesh and blood. They exist, but you can't see them with your naked eye. These enemies live within the corners of our minds and lurk in the alleyways of our thinking. They disguise themselves in the costumes of reason and logic. Who are they? What are they? What gives them their power?

Here are their names:

Ignorance
Laziness
Procrastination
Oppression
Low Self-esteem

Lack of Faith
Fear

These are powerful foes. Their voices aren't loud. They only need to whisper. They preach their destructive work in the classroom where a teacher tells a child: "You'll never learn." They can be heard in the home, when a parent tells a child: "You'll never amount to anything." They are woven into the society that believes the color of one's skin affects the quality of one's mentality. Their voices are the crooks of creativity, the burglars of bounty, the pickpockets of potential, and the purse-snatchers of purpose. They are the scavengers of men's souls.

Because of the whine of these voices, God has designed a quiet place set only to the frequency of His voice. He gave us a heart, not the blood-pumping muscle that keeps our bodies alive, but the space deep within our being that keeps who we are alive. It is here where God does His work.

So precious is this place—this sanctuary—this piece of hallowed ground—that God Himself has consecrated it by daring to abide there! It boggles the mind to think that God, the Master, the Supreme Being—He that *is* and ever more shall be—would desire to live within a human being.

> **ATTITUDE KEY**
>
> *An enemy will never tell you to stop working on your goal—he will merely whisper, "Do it tomorrow."*

God could live anywhere—and He does. He could dwell on Mt. Everest, St. Patrick's Cathedral, or the Taj Mahal. He would be welcome in the great temples of the world. No presidential palace, embassy, or religious shrine would refuse Him shelter. God dwells eternally as Ruler of all creation. Yet, the God of the universe desired to live in the likes of you and me!

ATTITUDE KEY
An enemy will never tell you to stop working on your goal—he will merely whisper, "Do it tomorrow."

God in me! Oh, if we only knew the value of the wealth buried inside of us. So valuable, so priceless is this wealth, that God himself stands guard over it. We are called God's field—God's garden. We are partakers and partners with Him. God doesn't desire to merely do things for us—He desires to do things *in* us—and ultimately *through* us. He wants to point at His creation and say, "Look at what they've accomplished . . . look at what they've done through faith in Me."

WHERE YOUR HEART IS

"Lay up for yourselves treasures in heaven... where your treasure is, there will your heart be also."

Deep within these words in Matthew 6, is a truth so liberating . . . so unshackling . . . so emancipating, that to grasp it's meaning is to change your world!
Think about it:

If your treasure is in heaven,
and your treasure is where your heart is—
then your heart is where heaven is.
And if heaven is in God,
And God is in your heart,
Then heaven is in your heart.

I no longer pray to be blessed. Neither do I complain when I think I haven't been blessed, because I am blessed! Why? Because I've been blessed from the day I was conceived—and this type of thinking has changed my entire outlook upon living!

No longer do I have to curse a system or society for not giving me what I feel it owes me. I don't have to be angry with the majority or status quo for not giving me a fair shake. I can move beyond them now. I don't need their permission to feel good about myself. And neither do you, if heaven's in your heart. We don't need the nod of controlling heads to sprint toward what belongs to us in this world. We have the right to achieve anything God has put in our hearts. No one person or group of people can hold us back. We have every gift necessary to propel us toward greatness—when heaven is in our hearts!

ATTITUDE KEY

Victory is the outcome of those who are willing to risk it all.

Chapter Eight

Blessings Out of Control

> . . . if I will not open you the windows of heaven, and
> pour you out a blessing, that there shall not be room
> enough to receive it . . .
>
> —Malachi 3:10

Words are the creative force of God. With words, God created the heavens and the earth. Words carry the plan, purpose, and intent of the one who speaks them. So if you want to know the plan, purpose, and intent of the Creator, listen to His words.

Notice God's phrase, ". . . if I will not open you the windows of heaven. . . ." Now isolate the words, "open *you* the windows. . . ." It appears as if the "you" in the passage "is" the windows of heaven. Yes, I know, I may be stretching it a bit. But if I were to take this away from the King James language and bring it into a modern translation, it would read, ". . . if I will not open the windows of heaven *for* you." That's what we expect to read. That's what we expect to happen. But could it be that the windows of heaven aren't *up* there, but down here *within* us? After all, the passage continues, ". . . and pour you out a blessing. . . ." It doesn't say and pour you *down* a blessing! If heaven is only *up there,* then we should expect blessings to come down. But this passage says *out.*

So the windows of heaven are very significant. They seem to be the control gate that regulates everything that flows from God. By opening them, all the wealth of God is released in a torrent flood!

I am the vine, ye are the branches . . .

—John 15:5

ATTITUDE KEY
Success is knowing where you're going, and having the assurance you'll get there—no matter what.

The Bible speaks of every believer as a branch connected to a vine. God is the vine and we are the branches connected to Him. We draw our strength, peace of mind, health, and providence from him. We are told that when we are connected to Him, we draw our needs from Him. So our source of anything we need is already there and available!

When we understand the flow of God in light of these principles, it's no wonder why we come to the conclusion that the windows of heaven are also within us. And considering again the phrase ". . . pour you out a blessing . . . ", could it be that we are the blessing that is to be poured out?

Jesus spoke of His life on earth as being ". . . poured out like water. . . ." The apostle Paul spoke of his life as a drink offering that was gradually being poured out over the span of his life.

Therefore, you and I are the blessing the world is waiting to receive because God put special gifts and talents within us that the world can't do without. Your personal wealth is connected to what is poured out of you. Do you think the world is willing to pay for a gift from God? You need to know they are!

Jesus told a woman as she came to draw water from a well one day that He would cause rivers of living water to "spring up out of her." From this account we can also understand that salvation, eternal life, healing, and victorious living all begin on the inside and erupt outward.

God always begins His work from within and moves outward. The Garden of Eden was just a small patch of ground in the midst of barren land. God's will for Adam and Eve was to extend the garden outward through their obedience and hard work. Of course, God would be with them—energizing and empowering them. But the work was to be done by them.

Once during a hiking trip, I noticed the pine trees along the trail. Several feet from the base of these trees were tiny seedlings and saplings. The seed from these trees fell and took root several feet from the base. Then as these new saplings grew to maturity, they too produced seed that would fall several feet from their base.

> **ATTITUDE KEY**
>
> *Finish what you started today—you'll thank yourself tomorrow.*

With every new generation, a forest's life cycle continues outward—taking more and more ground. This was God's plan for the garden of Eden. The seeds of creativity He planted in Adam and Eve were to flourish throughout the earth.

Each seed of God's talent, ability, and creativity is time released. At a specific moment in time, these seeds will come to maturity and explode to release His life in the generation they were timed to produce. There is more than one seed within you, *window of heaven.* Within you is not just one opening, one way of escape, or one window, but many!

ATTITUDE KEY

Fear is the brother of doubt, and doubt is the sister of unbelief. It's time to change families.

So don't allow frustration to seep in. God has you on automatic pilot! When your time comes, *nobody* will be able to stop you! Each sapling from the seed of God's tree of life is the future of mankind's forest. They may appear small and fragile at first, but just wait!

From the seeds within us, God pours us out more and more, extending out gifting and creativity further beyond our forest's edge—further beyond the bounds of where we started.

God's power, creativity, and passion is constantly flowing like the mighty Mississippi River, flowing from the north, down through the body of the United States. But He all too often flows around ignorant, hardened hearts, only to empty Himself into the vastness of the Gulf.

EXPECT YOUR FORTUNE FROM WITHIN

There is protocol—divine procedure. There is an attitude we must possess to make the most of all we have been given.

So first of all, expect your fortune in life to come from within. Don't look to someone else to provide what you already personally possess. Don't look to human flesh because people will either withhold things from you or discourage you from believing you deserve anything. So look within. If you are His, abiding in His vine, God is there! God is waiting! God is anxious to show you what He can do through you.

SEE YOURSELF AS A MAGNET FOR WEALTH

Second, see yourself from now on as a magnet for wealth. One of my hobbies is commodity trading. Each day I watch my charts, noticing the high volume of natural resources changing hands at an alarming rate. For every commodity that is bought, there must be a seller. So wealth is in the hands of people to acquire it, but it must come *from* or *through* people's hands.

People are drawn to happy, confident, secure people. People want to be around other people who enjoy life. Who wants to be around cynical people who are disgruntled with life? Not me! I'm quite sure you don't either!

Good attitudes start from within; they're born within people who are at peace with themselves. Who wouldn't rather sit beside a calm lake rather than a seething, raging river? So relax. Be confident. Be a magnet to people. With the coming of the right people will come wealth. You will attract it like bees to honey!

RELEASE YOUR GIFTS INTO THE WORLD AND THE WORLD WILL RELEASE IT'S WEALTH INTO YOU

The world is waiting for someone with a good idea—a better idea. It suffers acutely from a lack of innovation. Surges in the stock market tell us that people are willing to invest in someone with a good idea. As the saying goes, "Build a better mouse trap and the world will beat a path to your door."

How often we are led to believe that we're just like everyone else. This may produce humility, but it also suppresses the potential greatness within.

Did God break the mold when He made you? You bet He did! No one in this world has title to what He has given to you. Your thoughts and ideas are unique.

You are unique! So don't hold back. Let it go! And if you fail, you're in good company. Re-think: re-plan. Timing is everything. Try again! There's more of Him in you wanting to come out!

Chapter Nine

No More Room

> ... pour you out a blessing, that there shall not be room enough to receive it.
>
> —Malachi 3:10

We are channels for God and His flow never ceases. As rivers never start or stop, so it is with the wealth of God. There is no starting or stopping place. Just walls and dams—barriers erected to keep us from enjoying the perpetual flood of God's intentions.

God has designed a way for us to experience all that He has for us. He withholds nothing. He holds back nothing. He reserves nothing. He releases all we are capable of handling and using.

Imagine a pipeline. Now imagine this pipeline connected to the Omnipresent, Omniscient God who created you and all you can see. Imagine His wisdom, creativity, energy, strength, and ideas flowing to you through this pipeline. Imagine a constant, unlimited flow.

Now imagine if you will, an automatic shutoff

valve like the ones installed on the gasoline pump at your local gas station. When your automobile gas tank is full, the gas pump automatically shuts off. So it is with God's flow. The only thing that can stop the flow of His creativity and wealth is capacity or room. When the room is full, the flow stops, because God never wastes His resources.

> **ATTITUDE KEY**
>
> *There is a reason why you're on this planet—it's called purpose.*

Notice again the phrase in Malachi's passage, ". . . room enough. . . ." This implies there is dimension to the storage place of God's wealth. If there are dimensions, then it is possible for the room to expand. In the economy of God, each of us is given a reservoir, a storage place or room in which to contain His blessings. The dimension of the room is expandable.

A man's gift maketh room for him, and bringeth him before great men.

—Proverbs 18:16

Our gifts and talents define the dimensions of this room. The development of our abilities determines the size of the room. Our gifts and talents also bring us before great men. Therefore, our gifts and talents are in direct proportion to the size of our room. So, expand your gifts—expand your room. It's as simple as that!

DISCOVER YOUR GIFTS AND TALENTS AND YOU WILL DISCOVER GOD'S VEHICLE FOR YOUR SUCCESS

So discover your gifts and talents. Don't wait for

some prophet to tell you this! God will tell you. Start seeking and ask.

Ask yourself, *what is it that I do well? What is it I do that gives me joy? What is the thing I can do with ease that amazes others?* Don't seek to match the gifts of others. Their gift is their gift. Your gift is your gift. It will emerge. Expect it—look for it—wait for it!

DON'T BE AFRAID TO FAIL

Few have failed who didn't eventually succeed. The only way to discover your gifts and talents is through trial and error. So you've got to be willing to try and fail. Failure is never the end of your search, it merely tells you that what you've tried is not what God intends to use—at least not yet.

Failure is just a stop sign that gives you the opportunity to contemplate your next move. When viewed properly, it is only the comma in the continuation of your sentence—the continuation of your thought— the continuation of your search.

So be thankful for failure. For without it, you will never create your road map to success. You need to know where the mountains, valleys, roadblocks, and dead ends are positioned. Once you know where the obstacles are, you will know how to go around them.

> **ATTITUDE KEY**
>
> *Organization precedes the miraculous. So get organized.*

EXPAND YOUR ROOM

Since your gifts make room for you, it certainly

makes sense to develop them. Once you find the vehicle through which God desires to bless you, work on it—polish it up—study for it. Do you need more education? Go back to school. Find a seminar with professionals who know more about your vehicle than you do. Then go! Learn! Absorb!

> **ATTITUDE KEY**
>
> *Purpose is the key to prosperity.*

The development of your gift makes room for you. Filing down the rough edges of your talent makes room for you. Concentrating on what you do best expands your room. You may have to go to bed late and wake up early just to make time for making room. You may have to give up your spare time to make room. You may have to give up some play time or television time to make room. It doesn't matter. What's important, is that you make room! Whatever you must do to make room—do it! Your future depends upon it. Your family depends upon it. Your peace of mind and emotional welfare depends upon it. So do it!

MORE ROOM MEANS MORE BLESSINGS

As you develop more room, you create more space. Just as nature abhors a vacuum, so does God. God will fill up every inch of empty space you can create. The pipeline is open. The valve hasn't been shut off. The only thing that has kept additional blessings from flowing to your room—has been the size of your storage space.

There is no end to what God has to offer. Heaven carries unlimited resources. So don't look to the sky. The answer isn't there. Don't look to social programs—the answer isn't there. And don't look to friends or relatives to pity your cause—because the answer isn't there.

All the answer you need is hidden deep within the soil of your heart. Expect that soil to yield a harvest. Be reconciled to God through His Son Jesus, then trust God within you. For what He has placed within you will take you to heights unknown. Don't you know that your best days are yet to come?!

> **ATTITUDE KEY**
>
> *Whatever you choose to color your life with will be the picture that others see.*

Chapter Ten

The Power
of "One" Blessing

Now that we have considered the potential success of heaven in our hearts, we need to consider the power of God's blessing.

A few years ago I watched a movie featuring Billy Crystal called *City Slickers*. During a very comic moment, they were discussing the rewards of success. In this scene, one of the characters turned to Billy Crystal, lifted an index finger, and said, ". . . just *one thing*." He was referring to the fact that if you can find just *one* thing, and do it well, then you will be successful.

The Creator of the Universe promised to ". . . pour you out a blessing that there shall not be room enough to receive it." Notice that the pronoun in this statement which refers to God's blessing, "it" is singular, not plural.

> **ATTITUDE KEY**
>
> *God never gives you a vision without the provision.*

How fascinating! In other words, God has so much stored up for you, that He can bless you with just *one* blessing! He has placed such power in *one* seed, that the world can be conquered with just *one* idea!

THE SECRET OF BLESSING

For years, we've always thought of blessings as something tangible, something we can see, some thing we can touch. But we must remember that God is Spirit. He doesn't have a physical body. He exists in the spiritual realm. This tells us the blessings of God don't originate in the physical; they start in the Spirit.

> **ATTITUDE KEY**
>
> *Today when you stand before the mirror, remember that what you say affects the person you are looking at. So say something powerful.*

Everything that is created originates in the mind and imagination of someone. Whether you're building a house or a business, everything starts with an image. From that point, we seek to transfer that image onto paper. We design blueprints, develop a business proposal, or solicit an artist's rendering.

The image on paper is then given to the one who builds what they see. Material, tools, and labor are all included in the process. Finally, after all is done, we see the finished product.

What we see in our minds can be just as real as what we see with our eyes. How awesome is the power of perception. One thought, just one thought, can enable us to see ourselves as hideous or handsome, dreadful or desirable. One thought can make the difference between whether we complete a goal or give up too soon.

So, God doesn't need to flood us with many ideas. We only require one. One idea from God can give us wealth beyond our wildest dreams. And when I speak of wealth, I'm talking about the ability to have what you need, when you need it.

McDonalds, one of the largest and most successful food chains ever, concentrates on one thing. A recent independent study revealed that Burger King was slowly inching their way into the market that had been monopolized by McDonalds for years. So a fast food consultant was interviewed and asked what McDonalds needed to do to keep its share of the market. He said, "The answer is simple. McDonalds needs to stop trying to develop new products and concentrate on improving the products that brought them to this level of success."

Bill Gates of, Microsoft, the most successful software company of all time, has made billions fiddling around with computers. Of course he owns several other companies, but it's his software that made his fortune.

Each seed that God has planted in you is designed to support that one idea He desires to release into your life. Each seed is an open window of heaven, and when you decide to yield yourself to do what it takes to get those windows open, nothing, I mean nothing, will be able to stop you.

> **ATTITUDE KEY**
>
> *Forget yesterday and look forward to a brighter tomorrow.*

One blessing is so powerful, so potent, just one window in heaven isn't large enough to regulate the flow. God's one blessing will explode through every open space.

So it's up to you and me to go to work! If you want heaven in your heart to work through you—you must give heaven place.

DECIDE TO PUT GOD FIRST IN YOUR LIFE

So first of all, you're going to have to decide to give God first place. I've learned to start each new day by acknowledging God as the source of all I possess. I do this in two ways.

> **ATTITUDE KEY**
>
> *Forget yesterday and look forward to a brighter tomorrow.*

First, I wake each morning talking to God because I believe He is there with me. I thank Him for what He has already provided for me. Then I thank Him for the strength and ability He consistently infuses me with. I then acknowledge Him as overseer of all my plans and activities.

Secondly, I acknowledge God in a tangible way. For some of you, this area may be a little hard to digest. But this has worked to my benefit for years. I make sure that I give some of what He has blessed me with back. I've chosen to give at least 10 percent of my income to my church. They're doing a wonderful job building the creativity, courage, self-esteem, and faith of thousands of people. And there's nothing wrong in helping other people find what they possess. Many are discovering the place of heaven in their heart as a result of my church's outreach.

SEARCH FOR YOUR "ONE" BLESSING

Next, don't hesitate to pray, meditate, and ask God about your one blessing. Then look deep within and ask yourself: What do I love doing? What do I do well? What do I do with ease that other people find difficult? Then don't be afraid to ask your friends these same questions about yourself. Some may have insight. Others may not.

GO TO WORK

Finally, never forget that dreams and goals alone do not make a person successful! You have to do something about it. You say you don't have the time? *Make* the time! If you have to go to bed late and get up earlier than usual, make the time. Why? Because God makes us do nothing. But He will lead us into everything!

God directs our steps. But you must be stepping for God to direct them. Leave nothing to luck and chance. Don't wait for fortune to come to you, *go after it!* If there is no opportunity, make your own opportunity.

Someone once said, "Opportunity only knocks once." So if you've missed your knock, sit by someone else's door down the street until opportunity shows up again. Then bring it back to your door again! If heaven is in your heart and God's seeds are waiting to release—find a new field—give Him place—never give up—it's not too late! Get out of your box!

Battles aren't won on the front line. They're won in the strategy room, the place where Generals gather to plan. So take charge of your life. God has made you a General over your sphere of influence. Every battle won't be pretty. Some will be bloody and filled with retreats. There will be casualties. Expect the whispering enemies of fear and constant fire from the enemy's camp. Such is the nature of battle.

Finally, be of good courage and keep your head

up, even if you must cry. There will be wounds, hurt, and tragedy. Your body, mind, and emotions will ache from the scars you receive in battle. But be proud of your battle scars: they will be your medals. They will help you tell the story of how you won the war. And you *will* win once you climb out of your box, survey the horizon, and discover the genius God has placed within you!

There are no mistakes in life . . .

. . . only lessons.